AF270421

MIAMI

MARLINS

BY PATRICK DONNELLY

SportsZone

An Imprint of Abdo Publishing
abdobooks.com

abdobooks.com

Published by Abdo Publishing, a division of ABDO, PO Box 398166, Minneapolis, Minnesota 55439. Copyright © 2023 by Abdo Consulting Group, Inc. International copyrights reserved in all countries. No part of this book may be reproduced in any form without written permission from the publisher. SportsZone™ is a trademark and logo of Abdo Publishing.

Printed in the United States of America, North Mankato, Minnesota.
102022
012023

Cover Photo: Megan Briggs/Getty Images Sport/Getty Images
Interior Photos: Jonathan Daniel/Getty Images Sport/Getty Images, 4, 7; Pat Sullivan/AP Images, 9; Mitchell Layton/Getty Images Sport/Getty Images, 10; John Cordes/Icon Sportswire/Getty Images, 12; Hans Deryk/AP Images, 15; Andy Lyons/Getty Images Sport/Getty Images, 16; Timothy A. Clary/AFP/Getty Images, 21; Alan Diaz/AP Images, 22; Gary Hershorn/Pool/Getty Images Sport/Getty Images, 25; Eliot J. Schechter/Getty Images Sport/Getty Images, 27; Amy Sancetta/AP Images, 29; Jed Jacobsohn/Getty Images Sport/Getty Images, 31; Lynne Sladky/AP Images, 32; Wilfredo Lee/AP Images, 35; G. Fiume/Getty Images Sport/Getty Images, 37; Mike Ehrmann/Getty Images Sport/Getty Images, 38; Michael Reaves/Getty Images Sport/Getty Images, 41

Editor: Steph Giedd
Series Designer: Becky Daum

Library of Congress Control Number: 2022940486

Publisher's Cataloging-in-Publication Data

Names: Donnelly, Patrick, author.
Title: Miami Marlins / by Patrick Donnelly
Description: Minneapolis, Minnesota: Abdo Publishing, 2023 | Series: Inside MLB | Includes online resources and index.
Identifiers: ISBN 9781098290221 (lib. bdg.) | ISBN 9781098275426 (ebook)
Subjects: LCSH: Miami Marlins (Baseball team)--Juvenile literature. | Baseball teams--Juvenile literature. | Professional sports--Juvenile literature. | Sports franchises--Juvenile literature. | Major League Baseball (Organization)--Juvenile literature.
Classification: DDC 796.35764--dc23

CONTENTS

CHAPTER ONE
HERE COME THE MARLINS......4

CHAPTER TWO
FIVE-YEAR PLAN PAYS OFF ..12

CHAPTER THREE
BACK ON TOP 22

CHAPTER FOUR
TALENT AND TROUBLES........32

TIMELINE 42
TEAM FACTS 44
TEAM TRIVIA 45
GLOSSARY 46
MORE INFORMATION 47
ONLINE RESOURCES 47
INDEX 48
ABOUT THE AUTHOR 48

CHAPTER 1

HERE COME THE MARLINS

On a sunny, breezy October afternoon in Chicago, the Miami Marlins had a chance to break a long streak of frustration. The Marlins entered the 2020 season having missed the playoffs 16 straight years. Now they were one win away from winning their first playoff series since 2003.

The 2020 season was shortened due to the COVID-19 pandemic. Each team played just 60 games. And the top eight teams in each league made the playoffs. The Marlins were one of the eight from the National League (NL). They opened the playoffs with a best-of-three series against the Chicago Cubs.

Reliever Brandon Kintzler pitches in Game 2 of the wild-card series against the Chicago Cubs in 2020.

The Marlins surprised the Cubs in Game 1. Seventh-inning homers by Corey Dickerson and Jesús Aguilar drove in five runs. That was all Miami needed for a 5–1 victory.

The seventh inning was the Marlins' lucky charm again in Game 2. First baseman Garrett Cooper blasted a long home run to break a scoreless tie. Later in the inning, outfielder Magneuris Sierra singled home another run. That 2–0 lead lasted into the bottom of the ninth.

Miami reliever Brandon Kintzler stepped onto the mound, trying to close out the victory. But Chicago's Jason Heyward led off with a double. That meant the Cubs could tie the game with a home run. Kintzler faced the dangerous Javier Báez. After getting ahead in the count, Kintzler threw a fastball on the outside corner. Báez watched it go by for strike three.

Next up was slugger David Bote. Again, Kintzler got two strikes on the batter. And again, he threw a fastball on the outside corner that froze his opponent. Bote's strikeout left one batter to go. The Cubs turned to veteran Jason Kipnis to keep the game alive.

With the count two balls and two strikes, Kintzler reared back and fired. Clocking 93 miles per hour (150 km/h), the fastball caught the inside corner, just below Kipnis's hands. All he could manage was a feeble swing as the ball zoomed past him and into the catcher's mitt.

Kintzler had struck out the side, and the Marlins had won the first-round playoff series. It was their first postseason success since winning the World Series in 2003. And the young team was hungry for more.

BIRTH OF THE MARLINS

Major League Baseball (MLB) added two expansion teams in 1977, the Toronto Blue Jays and the Seattle Mariners. That brought the league's total to 26 teams, 14 in the American League (AL) and 12 in the NL.

Eventually, MLB decided to add two new NL teams too. Many cities applied to host one of the new teams. In June 1991, the league announced it would award the franchises to ownership groups based in Denver and Miami.

Marlins first baseman Garrett Cooper (26) celebrates after blasting a solo home run in Game 2 of the NL wild-card series.

The state of Florida was no stranger to professional baseball. MLB teams have visited cities throughout Florida for spring training since as far back as 1888. Most of those spring training sites are home to minor league teams during the summer.

However, Florida had never been represented by an MLB team of its own. Tampa-St. Petersburg built a domed stadium in the late 1980s in the hope that an existing MLB team would move there. Eventually, the market would get its own team, the Tampa Bay Rays. But the team based in Miami would be Florida's first. That's why the team was known as the Florida Marlins when it was formed. Marlins officials were hoping to make fans throughout the state, not just in Miami.

The team's ownership group was headed by H. Wayne Huizenga, a local businessman with an interest in sports. He was also a founding owner of the Florida Panthers. That team, also based in South Florida, began play in the National Hockey League in 1993. Huizenga later purchased a controlling interest

WHY THE MARLINS?

The Marlins' nickname is a nod to past minor league teams that had also used it. Other options were considered, including Manatees and Flamingos. But as owner Wayne Huizenga explained, "The marlin is slick, powerful, alert, agile and proud. It's a fierce fighter. . . . It can shake itself loose just when you think it's in trouble."

Pro Player Stadium offered plenty of seats but not the best experience for baseball fans.

of the Miami Dolphins of the National Football League in 1994, after being a minority owner since 1990.

Huizenga wasn't the Marlins' only link to the Dolphins. Miami lacked a baseball stadium suitable for MLB games. So the Marlins spent their first 19 years playing in the Dolphins' stadium. The empty seats at the massive football stadium tended to swallow even a big baseball crowd. And the

Marlins first baseman and left fielder Jeff Conine sports the team's signature teal uniforms before a 1993 game against the Chicago Cubs.

dimensions of the playing field were among the largest in the league, with the center field fence standing 434 feet (132 m) away.

Baseball traditionalists thought the ballpark was a bad fit for the sport. They were left scratching their heads again when they saw the Marlins' first set of uniforms. Until the early 1990s, professional sports uniforms were relatively conservative in design. Around that time, some teams in other sports began to use teal as their main color. But in baseball, most teams wore some combination of red, white, and blue.

The two expansion teams changed the baseball landscape with their color choices. The Colorado Rockies became the first MLB team to use purple as its primary color. And the Marlins hopped on the teal trend. The color tied the team to the Dolphins and emphasized its seaside location.

If the Marlins didn't look much like a big league ballclub, they didn't play like one very often either. The new teams built their rosters through an expansion draft. That meant most of their players were ones other teams didn't value highly enough to protect. As a result, the Marlins went 64–98 in 1993, finishing in sixth place out of seven teams in the NL East.

Things slowly got better in Miami. The team's winning percentage improved each of the next three years. The Marlins' 80–82 record in their fourth year was viewed as a sign of good things to come. But nobody could have predicted what the team would do in their fifth season.

FIVE-YEAR PLAN PAYS OFF

The young Marlins showed their potential in 1996. Right fielder Gary Sheffield broke out, hitting .314 with 42 homers and 120 runs batted in (RBIs). Steady left fielder Jeff Conine provided power and leadership. Shortstop Édgar Rentería, just 19 years old when the season began, hit .309 and played solid defense. He finished second in NL Rookie of the Year voting. And Charles Johnson won the second of four straight Gold Gloves as the best defensive catcher in the league.

On the mound, veterans Kevin Brown and Al Leiter combined for 33 victories and nearly 450 innings pitched. Leiter pitched the first no-hitter in team history on May 11

Marlins slugger Gary Sheffield preps for the pitch during the 1994 season.

against the Rockies. Closer Robb Nen posted 35 saves to lead a strong bullpen.

The 1997 season began with a new manager at the helm. Rene Lachemann, the Marlins' first manager, had been dismissed midway through the 1996 season. He was replaced to start the 1997 season with Jim Leyland. A gruff 52-year-old, Leyland had led the Pittsburgh Pirates to three division titles in the early 1990s.

Wayne Huizenga had given general manager Dave Dombrowski the green light to increase the team's payroll in hopes of reaching the postseason in their fifth year. That made it possible to sign third baseman Bobby Bonilla, outfielder Moisés Alou, and pitcher Alex Fernandez.

The upgraded Marlins started the season red hot. A 10–0 win over the Reds in Cincinnati on April 11 gave Florida an 8–1 record. The Marlins settled into second place in the East by the end of April. They stayed there pretty much the rest of the season. Brown no-hit the San Francisco Giants on June 10 for one of his 16 wins of the season. He joined Johnson and Alou in representing the Marlins at the All-Star Game in Cleveland that July.

Sheffield's numbers didn't match his amazing 1996 output, in part because a thumb injury he suffered in May nagged him all season. He did have one memorable moment though.

On July 14, he hit two homers in the same inning against the Philadelphia Phillies.

Newcomers Alou and Bonilla helped pick up the slack. Alou hit 23 homers and drove in 115 runs, while Bonilla added 17 home runs and 96 RBIs. Meanwhile, Fernandez led the team with 17 victories. All three free agents had a huge impact on their new team.

Moisés Alou played for the Marlins during the 1997 season. He was a six-time All-Star and two-time Silver Slugger over his career.

PLAYOFF BOUND

The Marlins finished the season 92–70. That was good enough to secure a wild-card spot by four games. Their first postseason appearance would kick off with a best-of-five NL Division Series (NLDS) against the Giants.

The Marlins won each of the first two games at home with a run in the bottom of the ninth. Rentería clinched the first win with a bases-loaded single. And Alou's base hit drove Sheffield

Liván Hernández pitches in the Marlins' Game 2 win against the San Francisco Giants in the 1997 NLDS.

home from second to win Game 2. The scene shifted to San Francisco for Game 3. Florida center fielder Devon White hit a grand slam in the sixth inning to lift the Marlins to a 6–2 win and a series sweep.

The Marlins moved on to face the strong Atlanta Braves in the NL Championship Series (NLCS). The Braves had won their division for six of the last seven seasons, this time with an MLB best 101 wins. After the teams split the first four games, Game 5 proved to be the turning point. The Marlins sent rookie Liván Hernández to the mound. He faced four-time Cy Young Award winner Greg Maddux of the Braves.

On paper it looked like a mismatch. But Hernández was ready for the challenge. He held the Braves to three hits and struck out 15 batters, an NLCS record. The Braves fumed all game, questioning home plate umpire Eric Gregg's strike zone. Many of the strikes called against Atlanta batters appeared to be well off the plate. That included the final pitch of the game to Braves slugger Fred McGriff. But all McGriff and his teammates could do was shake their heads as the Marlins celebrated a 2–1 victory. Florida clinched the series two days later with a 7–4 win in Game 6 at Atlanta.

BRING ON CLEVELAND

That set up a World Series showdown against the Cleveland Indians. Cleveland had three sluggers—Jim Thome, David Justice, and Matt Williams—who had hit at least 32 homers that season. Alou was the Marlin with the most home runs, at 23. But Florida had the edge on the mound. It would be a classic battle of strong pitching versus strong hitting.

Once again the teams split the first four games. The Marlins won Game 5, with Hernández pitching into the ninth inning.

Then Nen came in, getting the final three outs in an 8–7 victory. But Cleveland wouldn't go down easily, pulling out a 4–1 win in Game 6. That set up a winner-take-all Game 7 in Miami.

Leiter started for the Marlins and pitched well, allowing just two runs over six innings. But Cleveland's Jaret Wright pitched into the seventh and gave up just one run, a solo homer by Bonilla. The game reached the bottom of the ninth with Cleveland leading 2–1. Flame-throwing José Mesa came on to close out the game.

The Marlins had other ideas. Alou led off with a single. After Bonilla struck out, Johnson singled to right field. Alou raced to third base on the play. That brought up Craig Counsell.

Known more for his glove than his bat, Counsell had taken over the second base job in late July when rookie Luis Castillo was sent to the minors. He came through at the plate when it mattered. His line drive to right field was deep enough to drive in Alou from third. The sacrifice fly tied the game, keeping the Marlins alive.

The Florida bullpen kept Cleveland in check in the 10th and 11th. In the bottom of the 11th, the Marlins put together a rally. Bonilla led off with a single. One out later, Counsell hit a chopper to the right side of the infield. The ball scooted under second baseman Tony Fernández's glove and rolled into short right field. Bonilla made it all the way to third on the play.

Cleveland issued an intentional walk to Jim Eisenreich to load the bases. That set up a force-out at home plate. And that's exactly what Cleveland got. White hit a grounder to Fernández, and his throw beat Bonilla to the plate for the second out.

That brought up Rentería with the bases again loaded. The Marlins shortstop was just barely 21 years old at the time, the youngest player on either team. He was exactly who his teammates wanted to see at bat. That's because Rentería had driven in the winning run in the ninth or extra innings five times already that season. Cool as can be, Rentería stroked a line drive up the middle. It tipped off pitcher Charles Nagy's glove and rolled into center field. Counsell stomped on home plate, touching off a wild celebration. The Marlins, in just their fifth year, became the newest team in MLB history to win the World Series.

MR. MARLIN

Jeff Conine arrived in Miami in the November 1992 expansion draft. He'd played just 37 games in his MLB career, all for the Kansas City Royals. But he became known as "Mr. Marlin" after being selected to play in two All-Star Games and winning a World Series in his first five years in Miami. Conine was traded in the post–World Series fire sale. But the team brought him back during the 2003 pennant race, and he spent two more full seasons with the Marlins.

BREAKING UP THE GANG

The excitement didn't last long. Huizenga claimed that despite winning the World Series, the team had lost money that year. The Marlins had the second-highest payroll in the NL in 1997, and they finished fifth in the league in attendance. Still, Huizenga was convinced he had to cut expenses immediately.

Just two weeks after the World Series, the Marlins began making moves. Alou was traded to the Houston Astros. A week later, Nen was shipped to San Francisco and White to the Arizona Diamondbacks. Two days later, Conine—the last original Marlin—was sent to the Kansas City Royals. And in mid-December, Brown was traded to the San Diego Padres. In each case, Florida received minor leaguers in return for its star players. Only one of the prospects—first baseman Derrek Lee, acquired in the Brown deal—ever had any impact with the Marlins. This series of trades became known as "the fire sale."

The fire sale continued into 1998. Leiter was traded to the New York Mets in February. Finally, on May 14, 1998, the Marlins sent Bonilla, Sheffield, Johnson, and Eisenreich to the Los Angeles Dodgers. They did get All-Star catcher Mike Piazza in the deal. But they traded him to the Mets for more prospects a week later.

The fan reaction was to be expected. The Marlins fell to 13th of the 16 NL teams in attendance in 1998. And the team

Edgar Rentería, *top*, celebrates with his teammates after his game-winning hit in Game 7 of the 1997 World Series.

posted a dismal 54–108 record. Leyland resigned, and Huizenga sold the club to local businessman John Henry in the offseason. The Marlins would suffer through another extended stretch of losing as the frustrated front office struggled to build another winning team.

BACK ON TOP

In 2002 the Marlins went through another ownership change. John Henry wanted to buy the Boston Red Sox. He sold the Marlins to former Montreal Expos owner Jeffrey Loria. That seemed to bring new life to the team. Loria soon showed he was willing to invest in the roster again to bring a winner to South Florida.

During the streak of losing seasons following the World Series victory, the Marlins put together a new group of young talent. Those players would form the backbone of the Marlins' next winning team. The infield consisted of first baseman Derrek Lee, second baseman Luis Castillo, shortstop Álex González, and third baseman Mike Lowell. All were the

Dontrelle Willis, the 2003 NL Rookie of the Year, winds up to pitch against the Colorado Rockies.

regular starters by 2000. Lowell, at age 26, was the oldest of the quartet.

Two young right-handers, A. J. Burnett and Brad Penny, were gaining experience as starting pitchers. Josh Beckett, the number one pick of the 1999 MLB Draft, made his debut in 2001 and was a regular in the rotation the next year. A solid nucleus was forming. By 2003 the young Marlins were ready to win again.

The front office had made a few more moves in the years prior to rebuild the team. They added speed and a leadoff man by trading for center fielder Juan Pierre. Veterans Todd Hollandsworth and Juan Encarnación were brought in to play the corner outfield spots. Catcher Iván "Pudge" Rodríguez, a 10-time All-Star with the Texas Rangers, signed as a free agent.

The pitching staff added a few new faces as well. Rookie left-hander Dontrelle Willis arrived in a 2002 trade with the

LUIS CASTILLO

Chicago Cubs. Another seemingly minor deal brought former Detroit Tigers lefty Mark Redman to Miami. Beckett, Willis, Redman, and Penny joined right-hander Carl Pavano, who was gained in a 2002 trade.

Despite all these additions, the Marlins stumbled out of the gate in 2003. Slumping into May, they fired manager Jeff Torborg and turned the team over to Jack McKeon. The players responded to McKeon's leadership. It also helped when the 21-year-old Willis made his debut in May. The dynamic lefty took the league by storm. He stunned batters and charmed fans with his high leg kick and twisting windup. Willis won eight of his first 10 starts and went on to be named the NL Rookie of the Year.

In late July, the Marlins caught fire. They won nine of their last 10 games of the month to push their record to 59–49.

Carl Pavano pitched for the Marlins from 2002 to 2004.

With the strong pitching staff additions in recent years, the wins were adding up. Willis, Redman, and Penny would each win 14 games in 2003. Pavano added 12 more. Meanwhile Beckett, still just 23 years old, chipped in nine victories. Altogether they made up one of the steadiest rotations in baseball in recent years. However, nobody was going to catch the Atlanta Braves, who were on their way to another 101-win season. But the Marlins clinched the wild card in late September.

The team's chances appeared to take a hit on August 30 when Florida lost Lowell to a broken hand after he was hit by a pitch. He missed most of September. But the team hardly skipped a beat with the emergence of another rookie. Miguel Cabrera had just turned 20 when he made his debut with the Marlins that June. He played mostly left field. But he was adaptable enough to take over third base in Lowell's absence. He finished the year with 12 home runs and 62 RBIs in just 87 games. The Marlins also brought Jeff Conine back in a trade the day after Lowell was injured. He stepped into his familiar spot in left field.

As it did five years earlier, the path to the World Series began with an NLDS battle against the Giants. San Francisco won Game 1 at home. But the Marlins took the next three to advance. The lasting image of the series came on its final play. Conine threw out the potential tying run at home plate, and Rodríguez held onto the ball after a violent collision with San Francisco's J. T. Snow.

EXTENDING THE CURSE

This time, however, Florida's NLCS opponent would not be the Braves. They had been upset by the Chicago Cubs, who were trying to snap a long stretch of postseason slumps. The Cubs had last won the World Series in 1908. They were said to have been cursed by an angry fan in the 1945 season, the last time they had won the NL pennant. Now millions of Cubs fans throughout the country were ready to watch them reverse that curse.

It looked good for the Cubs as they took three of the first four games. Even after Beckett blanked them 4–0 in Game 5,

Catcher Iván Rodríguez holds on to the ball at home plate to make the final out of the 2003 NLDS.

TRADER JACK

hopes remained high. After all, the series returned to Wrigley Field, where the rowdy crowd was sure to put the home team over the top.

Indeed, Wrigley was rocking as the Cubs took a 3–0 lead into the eighth inning. Mark Prior, the Cubs' 23-year-old ace, had shut out the Marlins on three hits through seven innings. Chicago was just six outs away from returning to the World Series. Then it all unraveled.

Pierre hit a one-out double to give the Marlins a lifeline. Castillo followed with a fly ball down the left-field line. Former Marlin Moisés Alou, now playing left field for the Cubs, drifted to the wall and leaped for the foul ball. It bounced off the hands of a fan sitting in the front row. Alou was furious. He thought he could have made the catch and wanted fan interference called. The umpires disagreed, and Castillo's at-bat continued. He coaxed a walk from Prior, and Rodríguez followed with an RBI single.

The Cubs' Moisés Alou, a former Marlin, misses an out after a fan interfered during Game 6 of the 2003 NLCS. The Marlins went on to win Games 6 and 7 to advance to the World Series.

The rest of the inning was a nightmare for the Cubs. Lee tied the game with a two-run double that ended Prior's night. That came after a key error that—along with the disputed interference—could have ended the inning. Instead, the Marlins scored eight runs in the eighth and won 8–3.

The next night in Game 7, Cabrera's three-run homer in the first inning put the Marlins on top. The Cubs rallied to take a 5–3 lead. But the Marlins would not be denied. They silenced the crowd with three runs in the fifth and rolled to a 9–6 victory. The Cubs' curse remained unbroken, and the Marlins moved on to the World Series.

BOMBING THE BRONX

The New York Yankees were waiting for them. The core players of the Yankees' late-1990s dominant teams were still around. But they were starting to show their age. They had just survived a seven-game AL Championship Series with their rivals, the Boston Red Sox, to advance to face the Marlins.

Florida won Game 1 in New York. But the Yankees posted consecutive 6–1 wins in Games 2 and 3 to take control. When New York rallied for two runs in the ninth to tie Game 4, it appeared the Yankee magic might be too much for the Marlins. But the Florida bullpen got some big outs, and González led off the bottom of the 11th with a home run to tie the series.

That blow seemed to stagger the Yankees. Florida surged to a 6–1 lead in Game 5 and held on for a 6–4 victory. The series returned to Yankee Stadium for Game 6. The Marlins had

The Marlins' Jeff Conine slides into home plate to score on a sacrifice fly in their Game 6 win over the New York Yankees in the 2003 World Series.

already taken one game in the Bronx. They had every reason to be confident they could do it again.

Florida scored single runs off Yankees starter Andy Pettitte in the fifth and sixth innings. Meanwhile, Beckett rose to the occasion. On the game's biggest stage, the 23-year-old was pitching the game of his life. He locked down the Yankees all night. No New York runner even reached third base. And when Beckett fielded Jorge Posada's grounder and tagged out the Yankees catcher, the Marlins had a 2–0 win and their second World Series.

TALENT AND TROUBLES

The Marlins became well known for their fire sale after the 1997 World Series. The post–World Series drop-off wasn't as severe this time around, thanks to the young talent base the team had developed. But the Marlins muddled through the rest of the decade as basically a .500 team with just one second-place finish and no playoff appearances.

As this was happening, the team's approach began changing. Like Wayne Huizenga before him, Jeffrey Loria became concerned about the team's finances. He wanted a new baseball-only stadium. And until he could get that agreement in place, he started cutting the team's payroll. After the 2005 season, a number of veterans were allowed to leave

Hanley Ramírez rips a homer against the Cincinnati Reds in 2006. He went on to win the NL Rookie of the Year Award that season.

by free agency. The Marlins also traded Josh Beckett and Mike Lowell to the Red Sox. Luis Castillo and Juan Pierre were also traded for prospects. In the end, Loria had cut the payroll from $60 million to $15 million, by far the lowest in the league.

The cost-cutting did not end there. The best of the players to leave was Miguel Cabrera. Following his impressive debut in 2003, Cabrera developed into a superstar. He made the NL All-Star team in each of the next four seasons. Over that span, he averaged 32 home runs and 115 RBIs per season. He also became a consistent .300 hitter. And Cabrera was due a big payday after the 2007 season, so he and Willis were sent to the Detroit Tigers for another package of minor leaguers that offseason.

While the team was shedding payroll, it also added some talented young players. Shortstop Hanley Ramírez and right-hander Aníbal Sánchez, both gained in the Red Sox trade, emerged as future stars in 2006. Ramírez hit .292 with 17 homers and was named the NL Rookie of the Year. Sánchez made his debut in late June and went 10–3 with a 2.83 earned-run average (ERA) the rest of the way. He also pitched a no-hitter against the Arizona Diamondbacks on September 6. However, the Marlins were developing a reputation as a team capable of developing great players but not paying enough to keep them.

The Marlins' new stadium, Marlins Park, opened in 2012. It has a retractable roof.

Ramirez became the face of the franchise, hitting .342 to win the NL batting title in 2009. Slugging second baseman Dan Uggla averaged 31 home runs between 2006 and 2010. And hard-throwing right-hander Josh Johnson emerged as the team's new ace, winning 15 games in 2009 and posting an NL-best 2.30 ERA in 2010.

A NEW LOOK

Meanwhile, Loria finally had success in financing a new stadium. Marlins Park, a retractable-roof facility, was set to open in 2012. In the leadup to the move, the team underwent a rebranding, changing its name to the Miami Marlins and the team colors to a scheme incorporating orange, blue, yellow, silver, black, and white.

By the time the fresh-look Marlins moved into their new ballpark, a new slugger had emerged. Giancarlo Stanton hit 22 home runs in 100 games as a 20-year-old rookie in 2010. He became a fan favorite for his tape-measure shots. He hit 34 homers in his second season and 37 more in 2012, as he earned the first of four All-Star berths as a Marlin. Stanton won the NL home run crown with 37 in 2014. And in 2017, he had one of the best seasons in team history. Stanton blasted 59 homers, drove in 132 runs, and won the NL MVP Award.

SHOOTING STAR

In 2013 the Marlins welcomed the debut of 20-year-old pitching prospect José Fernández. The young right-hander quickly became a fan favorite. He played with an enthusiasm that

Giancarlo Stanton led the NL in home runs and RBIs on his way to winning the MVP Award in 2017.

Star Yankees shortstop Derek Jeter took over as CEO of the Marlins in 2017 until the start of the 2022 season.

matched his talent. He won the NL Rookie of the Year Award, going 12–6 with a 2.19 ERA. Injuries limited him to just 19 starts over the next two years, but he returned to form in 2016. Fernández earned his second All-Star appearance and went 16–8 with a 2.86 ERA. Tragically, that September, he was killed in a boating accident, robbing the baseball world of one of its most exciting young talents.

During the 2017 season, Stanton and the Marlins tried unsuccessfully to negotiate a new contract. Instead of letting him walk as a free agent the next year, the Marlins traded Stanton to the Yankees for three players. Again, the fans were disappointed that the team had failed to pay to keep one of its best players, especially because they hadn't had a winning season since 2009.

The front office also underwent major changes in 2017. That summer, Loria sold the team to a group led by businessman Bruce Sherman. One important member of Sherman's group was Hall of Famer Derek Jeter, the former Yankees shortstop. Jeter was named the team's CEO and put in charge of the team's day-to-day operations. He remained at that position until he stepped down before the 2022 season.

Another former Yankee great, Don Mattingly, took over as manager in 2016. He provided

GROUNDBREAKER

The Marlins made history in 2020 by making Kim Ng the first female general manager of a men's professional sports team in North America. She was also the first person of East Asian descent to run an MLB front office. A former softball player at the University of Chicago, Ng began her baseball career as an intern for the White Sox. Eventually, she worked in the front office for the White Sox, Yankees, and Dodgers. She also was the senior vice president of baseball operations for MLB.

stability after the Marlins had cycled through six managers in the previous six years. Mattingly was at the helm in 2020 when Miami made a surprise run to the playoffs. He was named the NL Manager of the Year for his efforts.

After beating the Chicago Cubs in the opening round of those 2020 playoffs, the Marlins were swept by the Braves in the NLDS. But young pitchers Sandy Alcántara, Trevor Rogers, and Pablo López and second baseman Jazz Chisholm gave Miami fans hope that their next surprise World Series appearance would be just around the corner.

Sandy Alcántara pitches for the Marlins during a 2022 game against the Washington Nationals in Miami.

TIMELINE

1991

South Florida is granted an expansion franchise by MLB.

1992

The Florida Marlins acquire 35 players in November's expansion draft.

1993

The Marlins draw more than 3 million fans in their inaugural season.

1997

Florida earns the NL wild-card spot, then takes over in the playoffs, defeating Cleveland in seven games to win its first World Series.

1998

After selling off much of their talent to cut costs, the Marlins crash-land at the bottom of the MLB standings with a 54–108 record.

2002

Luis Castillo sets a team record with a 35-game hitting streak and leads the majors in stolen bases for the second time with 48.

2003

The Marlins earn the wild card and roll through the postseason again, clinching the World Series on Josh Beckett's complete-game shutout at Yankee Stadium in Game 6.

2005

Lefty Dontrelle Willis wins 22 games and finishes second in NL Cy Young voting.

2006

Shortstop Hanley Ramírez wins the NL Rookie of the Year Award, and Joe Girardi is named NL Manager of the Year.

2007

Willis and Miguel Cabrera are traded to the Detroit Tigers at the end of the season.

2009

Outfielder Chris Coghlan is named the NL Rookie of the Year after hitting .321, while Ramírez hits .342 to win the NL batting title.

2012

The team rebrands itself as the Miami Marlins, changes its color scheme, and moves into its new ballpark.

2016

Pitcher José Fernández is tragically killed in a boating accident at Miami Beach. He was 24 years old.

2017

Giancarlo Stanton wins the NL MVP Award after hitting 59 homers and driving in 132 runs.

2020

The Marlins make a surprise playoff appearance and defeat the Cubs in a first-round playoff series.

TEAM FACTS

FRANCHISE HISTORY

Florida Marlins (1993–2011)
Miami Marlins (2012–)

WORLD SERIES CHAMPIONSHIPS

1997, 2003

KEY PLAYERS

Miguel Cabrera (2003–07)
Luis Castillo (1996–2005)
Jeff Conine (1993–97, 2003–05)
José Fernández (2013–16)
Álex González (1998–2005)
Charles Johnson (1994–98,
   2001–02)
Josh Johnson (2005–12)
Mike Lowell (1999–2005)
Hanley Ramírez (2006–12)
Gary Sheffield (1993–98)
Giancarlo Stanton (2010–17)
Dontrelle Willis (2003–07)

KEY MANAGERS

Rene Lachemann (1993–96)
Jim Leyland (1997–98)
Don Mattingly (2016–)
Jack McKeon (2003–05, 2011)

HOME STADIUMS

Sun Life Stadium (1993–2011)
   Also known as:
   Joe Robbie Stadium
      (1993–96)
   Pro Player Stadium
      (1997–2004)
   Dolphins Stadium (2005–06)
   Dolphin Stadium (2006–09)
   Land Shark Stadium (2009)
   Sun Life Stadium (2010–11)
loanDepot park (2021–)
   Also known as:
   Marlins Park (2012–20)

HAMMERING HOMERS

In 2008 the Marlins set a major league record with four infielders hitting at least 25 home runs. They were shortstop Hanley Ramírez (33), second baseman Dan Uggla (32), first baseman Mike Jacobs (32), and third baseman Jorge Cantú (29).

HOW THE MIGHTY HAVE FALLEN

The 1998 Marlins were the first team to lose 100 games one year after winning the World Series.

PINCH-SLAM

On August 31, 2005, the Marlins' Jeremy Hermida became the first player ever to hit a pinch-hit grand slam in his first MLB plate appearance.

A TRIBUTE TO FERNÁNDEZ

In the first game after his teammate José Fernández was killed in 2016, Miami's Dee Strange-Gordon led off the bottom of the first with a home run. He was wearing Fernández's helmet. It was just his ninth career home run in more than 2,000 at-bats.

DOWNSIZING

When the team moved into Marlins Park in 2012, the team had relocated from the largest stadium in baseball to the smallest. The park could seat only 37,000 fans compared to many ballparks that could seat more than 40,000 spectators.

GLOSSARY

ace
A team's best starting pitcher.

closer
A pitcher who comes in at the end of the game to secure a win for his team.

count
The number of balls and strikes on a batter during an at-bat.

expansion team
A brand-new team brought into an existing league.

franchise
A professional sports team, including the top-level team and all minor league affiliates.

free agent
A player whose rights are not owned by any team.

no-hitter
A complete game in which a team does not allow any hits.

pandemic
A widespread outbreak of a disease that affects a large portion of the population.

pennant
Another name for a league championship; in MLB, refers to winning either the American or National League.

sacrifice fly
A fly ball that a fielder catches for an out, but that results in a baserunner scoring.

shutout
A complete game in which a team allows no runs.

sweep
To win every game in a series.

MORE INFORMATION

BOOKS

Flynn, Brendan. *The MLB Encyclopedia*. Minneapolis, MN: Abdo Publishing, 2022.

Gitlin, Marty. *Great Baseball Debates*. Minneapolis, MN: Abdo Publishing, 2019.

Hewson, Anthony K. *GOATs of Baseball*. Minneapolis, MN: Abdo Publishing, 2022.

ONLINE RESOURCES

To learn more about the Miami Marlins, please visit **abdobooklinks.com** or scan this QR code. These links are routinely monitored and updated to provide the most current information available.

INDEX

Alcántara, Sandy, 40

Alou, Moisés, 14–15, 17–18, 20, 28

Beckett, Josh, 24–27, 31, 34

Bonilla, Bobby, 14–15, 18–20

Brown, Kevin, 13–14, 20

Cabrera, Miguel, 26, 30, 34

Castillo, Luis, 18, 23, 24, 28, 34

Conine, Jeff, 13, 19, 20, 26

Cooper, Garrett, 6

Counsell, Craig, 18–19

Fernandez, Alex, 14–15

Fernández, José, 36, 38

González, Álex, 23, 30

Hernández, Livan, 17

Hoffman, Trevor, 11

Huizenga, H. Wayne, 8–9, 14, 20–21, 33

Johnson, Charles, 13–14, 18, 20

Johnson, Josh, 35

Kintzler, Brandon, 6–7

Lachemann, Rene, 14

Lee, Derrek, 20, 23, 28

Leiter, Al, 13, 18, 20

Leyland, Jim, 14, 21

López, Pablo, 40

Loria, Jeffrey, 23, 33–34, 35, 36, 39

Lowell, Mike, 23–24, 26, 34

Mattingly, Don, 39–40

McKeon, Jack, 25, 28

Nen, Robb, 14, 18, 20

Ng, Kim, 39

Pavano, Carl, 25–26

Penny, Brad, 24–26

Pierre, Juan, 24, 28, 34

Ramírez, Hanley, 34–35

Redman, Mark, 25–26

Rentería, Édgar, 13, 15, 19

Rodríguez, Iván, 24, 27, 28

Sheffield, Gary, 11, 13–15, 16, 20

Stanton, Giancarlo, 36, 39

White, Devon, 16, 19, 20

Willis, Dontrelle, 24–26, 34

ABOUT THE AUTHOR

Patrick Donnelly is a freelance writer who lives in Minneapolis, Minnesota. He has covered Major League Baseball for more than 20 years.